impact

2
Grammar Book

T0349575

Australia · Brazil · Mexico · Singapore · United Kingdom · United States

impact

2
Grammar Book

Comparatives and superlatives

The

People celebrating Carnival in Rio de Janiero, Brazil

Comparatives and superlatives: Comparing two or more things

We use **adjectives** to describe nouns.
*Purple is a **popular** colour.*

We use the **comparative** form of the adjective to compare two people, animals or things. We often use the word *than* after the comparative form.
*Black is **darker than** pink.*

To make the comparative form of adjectives with one syllable, we add the ending *-er.*
green ⟶ *greener*

When the adjective ends in:
* -e, add *-r.*
white ⟶ *whiter*
* -y, take off the -y and add *-ier.*
tasty ⟶ *tastier*
* a vowel + consonant, double the last consonant and add *-er.*
red ⟶ *redder*

We use the word *more* with some two-syllable and with three-syllable (and longer) adjectives.
common ⟶ *more common*
popular ⟶ *more popular*

Some adjectives are irregular and do not follow these rules.
good ⟶ *better*
bad ⟶ *worse*

We use the **superlative** form to compare and rank three or more people, animals or things.
*Red is a **more popular** colour **than** green, but blue is **the most popular** colour in the world.*

To make the superlative form of adjectives with one syllable, we add the ending *-est.* We use the word *the* before the adjective.
green ⟶ *the greenest*

When the adjective ends in:
* -e, add *-st.*
blue ⟶ *bluest*
* -y, take off the -y and add *-iest.*
tasty ⟶ *tastiest*
* a vowel + consonant, double the last consonant and add *-est.*
red ⟶ *reddest*

1 Complete the sentences with the comparative form of the adjective in brackets.

Example: *Red grapes are **sweeter** than green grapes. (sweet)*

1. A pumpkin chilli is _____ than a raindrop chilli. (hot)
2. Brown bread is _____ than white bread. (healthy)
3. Green, leafy vegetables are _____ in iron than root vegetables. (rich)
4. I think home-cooked food is _____ than fast food. (delicious)
5. Your diet is probably _____ than mine. (varied)
6. Vegetable oils are _____ for you than butter. (good)
7. Blue food is _____ than green food. (unusual)
8. Dad's cooking is _____ than Mum's! (bad)

2 Complete the sentences with the superlative form of the adjective in brackets.

Example: *Meringues are **the sweetest** food I have ever tasted! (sweet)*

1. A *naga* chilli is _____ in the world. (hot)
2. Some people believe the Mediterranean diet is _____. (healthy)
3. My dad's chocolate pudding is _____ thing ever! (rich)
4. I think my mum's cooking is _____ of all! (delicious)
5. Lemons are _____ fruit I have eaten. (sour)
6. Milk chocolate is good, but dark chocolate is _____! (good)
7. Blue foods are _____ foods. (unusual)
8. My cooking is _____ in our family. I burn everything! (bad)

3 Complete the questions and sentences with the comparative or superlative.

Example: *Who eats **the healthiest** diet in your family? (healthy)*

1. Who bakes _____ cakes, you or your sister? (good)
2. Do you eat _____ your sister? (fast)
3. Which food is _____? Dark chocolate or caramel? (sweet)
4. A lot of people like coffee, but tea is _____ drink in the UK. (popular)
5. What is _____ thing you have ever tasted? (delicious)
6. What was _____ meal you ever had? (bad)
7. I am even _____ I was yesterday! (hungry)
8. In Asia, it is _____ to eat rice than pasta. (common)

The is the definite article. We use it:
- with singular and plural countable nouns and with uncountable nouns.

The cup is green.

The cups are green.

The coffee in the cup is warm.
- when we are talking about something specific.

*The cup of coffee that you bought is on **the** counter.*
- when we are talking about something which is unique.

*The best coffee shop is in **the** city centre. I go there when **the** sun is shining.*
- before the superlative form of adjectives and adverbs.

*It is **the** tastiest coffee in town.*
- with the names of some things, places, people, etc. (typically: family names made plural, regions, oceans, rivers, mountain ranges).

*It comes from **the** foothills of **the** Andes in Colombia.*

*It is grown by **the** Ramón family.*

A/An is the indefinite article. We use it:
- when we are talking about something that is not specific.

*Can I have **a** sandwich, please?*
- when we are talking about something for the first time.

*She's **a** chef.*

1   **Complete the sentences with *the* or *a/an*.**

Example: ***The** colour gold is associated with wealth.*

1. Red is _____ colour in the Chinese flag.

2. _____ Paraná river is in South America.

3. Most people think green is _____ colour of nature.

4. There is _____ blue butterfly in _____ garden.

5. Blue is _____ colour of the sea and the sky.

6. Purple is _____ interesting colour, often associated with royalty.

7. Eight per cent of _____ population is red–green colour blind.

8. _____ green and orange vase is beautiful.

2 Read. (Circle) the correct option.

Example: *Every afternoon, he ate* **the** / (**a**) *chocolate bar.*

1. The bird we can hear is in **the** / **a** tree above us.

2. **The** / **A** train left before I arrived at the station.

3. I live in **the** / **an** enormous house in the countryside.

4. We spend time in **the** / **a** city at weekends.

5. I saw you on **the** / **a** television last night!

6. I have entered a competition to win **the** / **a** holiday.

7. After you told me about it, I entered **the** / **a** competition.

8. Do you know what **the** / **a** time is?

3 **Are these sentences correct?** Tick the correct sentences. Rewrite the incorrect sentences.

Example: *The actor in a film was amazing!*
        The actor in **the** *film was amazing!*

1. There is the shop at the end of the road.

_____

2. Orange is the warm colour.

_____

3. The grey seal is bigger than the common seal.

_____

4. You can have a green salad if you're not hungry.

_____

5. Red is the colour that means different things to different people.

_____

6. Black is a mysterious colour.

_____

7. Strawberries are a tastiest fruit.

_____

8. A sea is blue.

_____

WRITING

Research and write five sentences on how different colours were used throughout history.
Use comparatives and superlatives.

Examples: *Titian used* **the brightest** *blue colour in his paintings.*
        Roman emperors wore **the most expensive** *purple cloaks.*

Adverbs
Make + adjective

Girls on bikes in Mandalay, Myanmar

Adverbs: Saying how and how often you do something

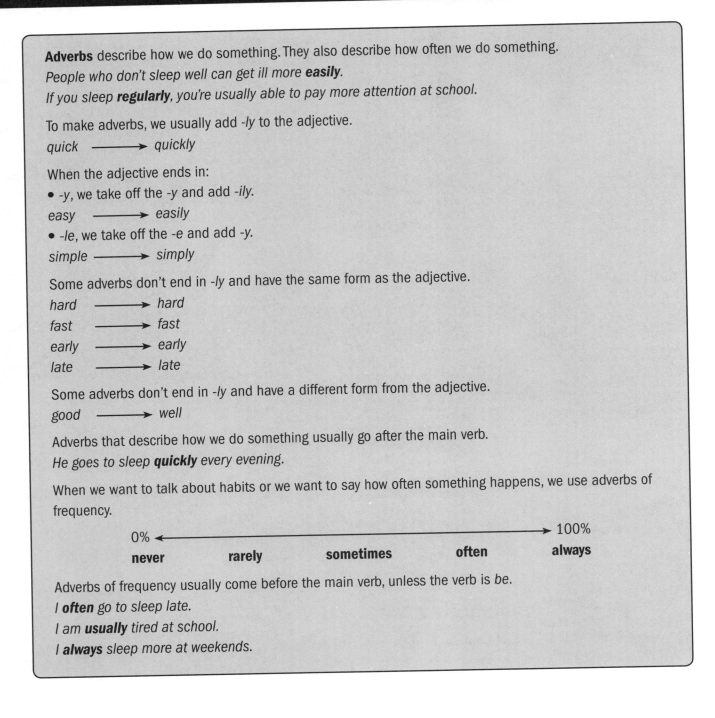

Adverbs describe how we do something. They also describe how often we do something.

*People who don't sleep well can get ill more **easily**.*

*If you sleep **regularly**, you're usually able to pay more attention at school.*

To make adverbs, we usually add -ly to the adjective.

quick ⟶ quickly

When the adjective ends in:

• -y, we take off the -y and add -ily.

easy ⟶ easily

• -le, we take off the -e and add -y.

simple ⟶ simply

Some adverbs don't end in -ly and have the same form as the adjective.

hard ⟶ hard

fast ⟶ fast

early ⟶ early

late ⟶ late

Some adverbs don't end in -ly and have a different form from the adjective.

good ⟶ well

Adverbs that describe how we do something usually go after the main verb.

*He goes to sleep **quickly** every evening.*

When we want to talk about habits or we want to say how often something happens, we use adverbs of frequency.

0% ⟵————————————⟶ 100%

never　　**rarely**　　**sometimes**　　**often**　　**always**

Adverbs of frequency usually come before the main verb, unless the verb is *be*.

*I **often** go to sleep late.*

*I am **usually** tired at school.*

*I **always** sleep more at weekends.*

1 **Complete the sentences with an adverb from the box.**

| badly | carefully | easily | late | often | quickly | ~~rarely~~ | regularly | well |

Example: I **rarely** go to bed before midnight.

1. I slept very _____ last night and feel great this morning.

2. He _____ completed the test in time.

3. I watched as the boy _____ picked up the injured bird.

4. I arrived _____ and the play had started.

5. The girls played _____ and lost the match.

6. If you take the medicine, you will get better _____.

7. It's important to exercise _____.

8. Jason _____ goes to the library after school.

2 **Complete the second sentence so it has the same meaning as the first.**

Example: It is a fast train. The train travels **fast**.

1. My sleep is good. I sleep _____.

2. My food is healthy. I eat _____.

3. He was gentle when he touched the bird. He touched the bird _____.

4. My dad was very angry. He reacted _____.

5. My test result was terrible. I did _____ in the test.

6. My sister was calm during the storm. She behaved _____.

7. My teacher was clear when she explained the topic. She explained the topic _____.

8. It isn't usual for me to go to bed after midnight. I don't _____ go to bed after midnight.

3 **Use the prompts to write questions.** Change the adjectives to adverbs.

Example: your brother / sleep / good   **Does your brother sleep well?**

1. he / go to bed / early _____

2. why / your sister / sleep / bad _____

3. how / you / think / clear _____

4. why / you / talk / loud _____

5. why / you / eat / slow _____

6. when / we / learn / quick / in class _____

7. what / you / do / frequent _____

8. when / I / get up / easy _____

Make + adjective: Saying what affects mood and feelings

The verb *make* + **adjective** is used with mood and feelings. We use it to describe how someone or a group of people feels as a result of something else.

*A lack of sleep **makes** you tired.*

*Some viruses **make** us very ill.*

Subject pronouns	I	you	he/she/it	we	you	they
Object pronouns	me	you	him/her/it	us	you	them

1 **Complete the sentences with *make* or *makes* and the object pronoun in brackets.**

Example: *Exercise usually **makes me** feel good. (I)*

1. Sleeping well _____ calmer. (we)

2. Being late _____ angry. (she)

3. Some viruses _____ very weak. (you)

4. Medicine _____ feel better. (we)

5. Exams _____ nervous. (I)

6. Sunshine and rain _____ grow quickly. (it)

7. Mum says that a healthy diet _____ more resistant to illness. (we)

8. I do it to _____ happy. (they)

2 **Match the two halves to make complete sentences.**

1. Medicine usually   a. makes me happy.

2. Lying in the sun can   b. makes me nervous.

3. Eating too much fast food can   c. makes us feel better.

4. Watching my football team score d. make you feel hot.

5. Speaking in front of a lot of people e. often makes people feel calmer.

6. Really loud music can   f. make you fat.

7. A lovely, warm bath   g. make your skin turn blue.

8. Very cold water can   h. sometimes make my head hurt.

3 Rewrite the sentences in the negative.

Example: *Fast food makes me ill.*
*Fast food **doesn't make** me ill.*

1. A bad night's sleep makes me happy.

   _____

2. Exercise makes us feel worse.

   _____

3. My friends make me sad.

   _____

4. My mum makes me wash my own clothes.

   _____

5. My dad makes me play football when I'm tired.

   _____

6. My brothers make me angry.

   _____

7. Homework makes my friends stressed.

   _____

8. Listening to music makes me feel sad.

   _____

4 Complete the sentences with your own ideas.

Example: ***Swimming in the sea** makes me cold.*

1. _____ makes me ill.
2. _____ makes me happy.
3. _____ makes me angry.
4. _____ makes me sad.
5. _____ makes me tired.
6. _____ makes me laugh.
7. _____ makes me cry.
8. _____ makes me nervous.

WRITING

Write three sentences saying how often people make you feel a certain way.

Example: *My sister **often makes me** feel annoyed.*

Modals

Must, might and *can't*

This girl is wearing a high-tech armband that can find her friends nearby, send text messages and even act as a video-game controller.

Modals: Expressing obligation, advice and permission

We use **modal** verbs to express:

- obligation, both affirmative and negative.

*Students **don't have to** ask to use the computer, but they **must** ask if they can go online.*

- advice, both affirmative and negative.

*You **should** be careful about your safety online. You **shouldn't** give away personal information. You **have to** protect yourself with a strong username and password.*

- permission, both affirmative and negative.

***Can** anyone use the computer at the library? You **can/may** only use the Internet if you have a library card. Children under 14 **can't/may not** use the Internet at all.*

➔ See grammar box on page 52.

1 **Write advice or rules for each situation.**

Example: *I haven't changed my password for years. (change / password / urgently)*
    You should change your password urgently.

1. I'm not allowed to watch this film. (be / 15 years old)

   _____

2. He is choosing a new password. (not be / easy to guess)

   _____

3. You can't afford the new game. (buy / something else)

   _____

4. We have to be polite. (not be / rude)

   _____

5. I want to post photos of friends online. (ask / their permission)

   _____

6. They want to design their own website. (ask / IT teacher)

   _____

7. You are bullied online. (talk / friends and family)

   _____

8. I am joining a new site. (choose / password carefully)

   _____

2 **Complete the sentences with *should, must* or *can.* Use the affirmative (+) or negative (-) form.**

Example: *My friend says I **should** change my password. (+/advice)*

1. They _____ go online during exams. (-/rule)
2. You _____ try reading books online. (+/advice)
3. My younger brother _____ go online when he asks. (+/permission)
4. The restaurant _____ take online bookings. (+/advice)
5. People _____ respect each other in this chat room. (+/rule)
6. Going online _____ be the only thing we do in our free time. (-/advice)
7. My sister _____ use the Internet after midnight at home. (-/permission)
8. She _____ complain. (-/advice)

3 **Complete the sentences with *have to* or *may.* Use the affirmative (+) or negative (-) form.**

Example: *You **don't have to** wear a uniform to school. (-/obligation)*

1. Students _____ go to the shops at lunchtime. (-/permission)
2. Students _____ talk in the exam hall. (-/permission)
3. We _____ use a blue pen. (-/obligation)
4. He _____ leave the room if he finishes early. (+/permission)
5. The school _____ close at 7 p.m. (+/obligation)
6. Students _____ leave before 7 p.m. (+/permission)
7. The head teacher _____ come into your class at any time. (+/permission)
8. We _____ be quiet during school assemblies. (+/obligation)

4 **Is this obligation (O), advice (A) or permission (P)? Write O, A or P.**

Example: *You must not talk in class.*   <u>**O**</u>

1. You should not talk in class.   _____
2. You may discuss this with your classmates now.   _____
3. You should write in ink – it's clearer.   _____
4. You must write in black ink.   _____
5. You may use a dictionary.   _____
6. You should dress smartly for school.   _____
7. You must not wear jewellery in school.   _____
8. You have to greet your teacher every morning.   _____

Must, *might* and *can't* are modal verbs. They are followed by a bare infinitive.

Must expresses certainty that something has happened or is true.
I checked these facts on three different websites, so they must be true.

Might expresses a lack of certainty that something has happened or is true, but that it is possible.
This might be her social media page. I'm not sure.

Can't expresses strong doubt that something has happened or is true, or even a certainty that it hasn't happened or isn't true.
He can't be the author of this article: he doesn't know anything about the topic!

➔ See grammar box on page 52.

1 **Say if the statements are likely (L) or unlikely (U).** Write L or U.

Example: *Sperm whales can hold their breath for 90 minutes.*   __L__

1. Athletes spend 168 hours a week training.   _____

2. The deadliest animal in Africa is the hippopotamus.   _____

3. Cats sleep 18 hours a day.   _____

4. I can hold my breath for 16 minutes.   _____

5. It takes an hour to fly from London to New York.   _____

6. Your friend's dad has got a pet crocodile.   _____

7. Computers can beat humans at chess.   _____

8. My grandmother is 124 years old.   _____

2 **Match the responses to the statements in Activity 1.**

Example: *That must be true! They can dive really deep.*   **Example**

1. That can't be true. It takes at least five hours.   _____

2. That might be true. They are very advanced.   _____

3. That must be true. My cat is always asleep!   _____

4. That might be true. They are big and aggressive.   _____

5. That can't be true. They're too big to be pets.   _____

6. That can't be true. Humans have to breathe!   _____

7. That can't be true. The oldest human ever was 122!   _____

8. That can't be true. There are only 168 hours in a week!   _____

3 **Read.** (Circle) the correct option.

Example: *The sun is rising. It* **might** / (**must**) *be morning!*

1. The sky is grey. It **might** / **must** be raining.

2. It's been freezing all night. The ground **can't** / **might** be icy.

3. I **mustn't** / **can't** believe that you don't own a smartphone.

4. My computer just went off! There **must** / **can't** be a power cut.

5. The other team look good, but we **might** / **can't** win.

6. We **might** / **must** leave now, otherwise we'll miss the train.

7. If they're not here, it **can't** / **must** mean that they're delayed.

8. They are practising really hard. They **can't** / **must** be expecting a tough match.

4 **Tick the correct sentence.**

Example: ☐ a. *We may to go to the fast food restaurant.*

☑ b. *We may go to the fast food restaurant.*

1. ☐ a. It might to be true that elephants have long memories.

☐ b. It must be true that elephants have long memories.

2. ☐ a. He said he was hungry. He must want something to eat now.

☐ b. He said he was hungry. He can't want something to eat now.

3. ☐ a. You love pizza, so you must like Italian restaurants.

☐ b. You love pizza, so you can't like Italian restaurants.

4. ☐ a. It can't be expensive to travel first class.

☐ b. It must be expensive to travel first class.

5. ☐ a. I can't go to the cinema tomorrow. Are you coming?

☐ b. I might go to the cinema tomorrow. Are you coming?

6. ☐ a. She must be good at French – she *is* French!

☐ b. She might be good at French – she *is* French!

7. ☐ a. That's too much money! You can't be serious!

☐ b. That's too much money! You can't to be serious!

8. ☐ a. We must believe everything we read online.

☐ b. We can't believe everything we read online.

Used to and *would*

Past simple

Exploring a shipwreck near Key Largo, Florida, USA

Used to and *would*: Talking about habits in the past

We use **used to** and **would** to describe past habits (i.e. things done regularly). They are both followed by a bare infinitive.

We use **used to** to talk about:

• things that happened often in the past but that don't happen now.

*I **used to** read every day!*

• situations that existed in the past but that don't exist now.

*We **used to** live by the sea, but now we live in the city.*

The negative and question form is *use to*, not *used to*.

*I **didn't use to** read much at all!*

***Did** you **use to** read about the sea as a child?*

We also use **would** to talk about things that happened often in the past but that don't happen now.

Would is slightly more formal than **used to**.

*During the summer, we **would** spend our days on the beach.* OR *During the summer, we **used to** spend our days on the beach.*

We don't use **would** to talk about past situations or states. We use **used to**.

*My dad **used to** be a diver, but now he is retired.* NOT *My dad **would** be a diver, but now he is retired.*

---

1 **Are the words in bold correct?** Tick the correct sentences. Rewrite the incorrect words.

Example: *We **used to** watch a lot of documentaries when we were young.* ✔

1. My uncle **would** live in Kenya. _____

2. Every morning, we **would** watch the fishing boats in the harbour. _____

3. When he was young, Mr Graham **would** be a teacher. _____

4. I never **used to** like swimming underwater. _____

5. My mum **would** often go shopping on a Saturday morning. _____

6. We **would** live in a small village when I was young. _____

7. At night, my older brother **would** tell me scary stories. _____

8. My grandfather **would** have a pet dog called Topper. _____

2 **Complete the article with *used to* or *would*.** In some cases, either might be correct.

When we were little, my brother and I _____used to_____ pretend to be explorers.

We ¹_____ live in the city and we didn't have a garden. We ²_____

go to the local park and we ³_____ pretend that it was a big forest. Our mum

⁴_____ be the park ranger although she never ⁵_____ come with us!

My brother ⁶_____ find sticks and pretend they were exotic snakes. We had great fun,

and we ⁷_____ always go home with stories to tell our parents.

3 **Rewrite the sentences using *used to* or *would*.**

Example: *My grandfather was a pilot.*
My grandfather used to be a pilot.

1. There were propeller planes before jet airlines.

   _____

2. With propeller planes, there were more stops on routes.

   _____

3. My grandfather flew regularly to Asia.

   _____

4. On every trip, there were four or five stops.

   _____

5. The flight from London to Singapore took nearly three days.

   _____

6. It stopped in Sicily, Alexandria, Basra and Karachi.

   _____

7. Flying was a big adventure.

   _____

8. It was also very expensive. Only very wealthy people flew.

   _____

4 **Are these past habits (H), situations (S) or both (B)?** Write H, S or B.

Example: *There were no wetsuits before the 1950s.*   **S**

1. Instead of wetsuits, surfers wore wool suits coated in oil.   _____
2. They only spent a few minutes in the water.   _____
3. My grandfather surfed every weekend.   _____
4. He and his friends lived by the sea.   _____
5. Surfing was only popular in Hawaii.   _____
6. Most people in England weren't interested in surfing.   _____
7. Before wetsuits, divers wore heavy diving suits.   _____
8. It was very difficult to move in the water.   _____

We use the **past simple** to talk about past actions, such as:

• things that started and finished in the past.

*Last October, divers **discovered** a shipwreck in the Indian Ocean.*

*Nautilus **reached** the Gulf of Mexico **the day before yesterday**.*

• things in the past which were habits or happened often.

*A **hundred years ago**, passenger ships **sailed** across the Atlantic every day. They also **carried** cargo.*

• things in the past which happened (or didn't) one after the other.

*In **1912**, RMS Titanic **set off** from Southampton, UK. The ship **didn't arrive** at its destination.*

We form the past simple affirmative of regular verbs by adding the -ed ending.

discover ⟶ discovered

When the verb ends in -e, we add -d.

arrive ⟶ arrived

When the verb ends in a consonant and -y, we take off the -y and add -ied.

carry ⟶ carried

We often use time expressions with the past simple. These can come at the beginning or the end of the sentence.

Last year, I flew to Brazil.

I went to Argentina in 2016.

➔ See grammar box on page 52.

Some verbs are irregular, e.g. *go*:

*Where **did** you **go** yesterday? I **went** to the library.*

➔ See the irregular verbs list on page 55.

---

1 **Complete the text with the past simple of the verbs in brackets.**

Last week, I _____saw_____ (see) a great documentary. It [1]_____ (be) about how people [2]_____ (discover) the *Titanic*. I [3]_____ (know) some of the things they [4]_____ (talk) about in the programme, but I [5]_____ (not know) that finding it was so difficult. The explorers [6]_____ (search) an enormous area of the seabed. They finally [7]_____ (find) the wreck 1,000 miles east of Boston, and [8]_____ (take) the first photos of it in over 70 years.

2 **Read the answers.** Write the questions.

Example: *What **did Robert Ballard find**?*
   He found the wreck of the Titanic.

1. When _____?
   He discovered the wreck in 1985.

2. Where _____?
   He discovered it about 1,000 miles east of Boston.

3. How _____?
   The *Titanic* was about 12,000 feet deep.

4. What _____?
   They first photographed one of the ship's boilers.

5. Where _____?
   The boiler was in the sand on the sea floor.

6. When _____?
   James Cameron reached the wreck in 2012.

3 **Change the sentences from affirmative to negative.**

Example: *It took him a long time to find the wreck.*
   It didn't take him a long time to find the wreck.

1. I wrote an article about the expedition.

   _____

2. He stole many artefacts.

   _____

3. He discovered the wreck in 2004.

   _____

4. It caused lots of damage.

   _____

5. The divers lost many items.

   _____

6. He wanted to become an explorer when he was young.

   _____

WRITING

Write a short review of a history programme you have seen. Explain what it was about. Try to include:

1. what the presenters did during the programme (past simple).

2. details of what the subject of the programme used to do (past habits).

Example: *The presenters **explored** the landscape around Stonehenge. They **described** the ceremonies the ancient Britons **used to take part** in.*

Present perfect

As ... as

Kevin Hand works in extreme environments.

Present perfect: Describing past experiences that connect to the present

We use the **present perfect** to talk about:

* something that just happened.

I **have just finished** a book about space travel.

* something that happened in the past but has a connection with the present.

I **have read** the book, so I can tell you all about it.

* things that happened in the past but with no clear timeframe.

A large proportion of the Earth's surface **has been explored**.

* something that started in the past but has not finished.

He **has worked** in this field since 1999.

* our own experience, or lack of it.

I **have studied** many extreme environments, but I**'ve never been** to Antarctica.

* other peoples' experience, or lack of it.

Have you **ever seen** a giant tube worm?

* something that happened in the past but has a connection with the present.

The study of extremophiles **has taught** us a lot about the origins of life on Earth.

The past participle of irregular verbs is NOT formed with the ending -ed. We form the past participle of these verbs in different ways.

do ⟶ did ⟶ done
begin ⟶ began ⟶ begun

➔ See grammar box on page 52.

REMEMBER

The verb go has two past participles: gone and been.

We use have/has gone to say that someone has gone somewhere and has not come back yet.
He has **gone** to Antarctica.

We use have/has been to say that someone went somewhere and has come back.
He has **been** to Antarctica.

1 **Complete the sentences with the negative form of the present perfect.**

Example: I **haven't finished** my research on glaciers. (finish)

1. The scientists _____ the data fully yet. (analyse)

2. They _____ any evidence. (find)

3. My colleague _____ his research. (publish)

4. We _____ on to the next stage of the project. (move)

5. She _____ hope of starting next year. (give up)

6. The government _____ putting pressure on them. (stop)

7. The stress _____ easy to live with. (be)

8. We _____ here to disturb you. (come)

2 **Use the prompts to write questions in the present perfect.**

Example: you / go / extreme environment   **Have you been to an extreme environment?**

1. I / study / this subject before   _____

2. they / finish / their research   _____

3. what / you / decide /about / your project _____

4. how / you / raise money for research   _____

5. we / come / to any conclusions   _____

6. what / gadgets / scientists / develop _____

7. what / animals / biologists / study   _____

8. what / information / you / find   _____

3 **Use the prompts to write sentences about yourself in the present perfect.**

Example: hottest place / ever / be   **The hottest place I've ever been is the Sahara Desert.**

1. busiest city / ever / go   _____

2. largest animal / ever / see   _____

3. most beautiful place / ever / visit _____

4. longest journey / ever / made   _____

5. highest mountain / ever / climb   _____

6. coldest water / ever / swim in   _____

7. most interesting book / read / this year _____

8. worst film / see / this month   _____

As ... as: Making comparisons of equality

We can compare two similar things using **as ... as**.
We can use it with an adjective.
*The Pacific hagfish is just **as important as** other fish.*
We can use it with an adverb.
*Polar bears can't swim **as fast as** penguins.*
We can use it with a quantifier.
*Humans have **as many hairs on their bodies as** chimpanzees.*
*The blue whale weighs **as much as** 23 elephants!*

1 **Complete the sentences using *as ... as*.**

Example: *African elephants are bigger than Asian elephants.*
        *Asian elephants aren't **as big as** African elephants.*

1. Pacific hagfish can swim deeper than sperm whales.

   Sperm whales can't swim _____ Pacific hagfish.

2. A newborn giraffe is lighter than a newborn elephant.

   A newborn giraffe isn't _____ a newborn elephant.

3. Chimpanzees are smaller than gorillas.

   Chimpanzees aren't _____ gorillas.

4. Mako sharks are faster than great white sharks.

   Great white sharks can't swim _____ mako sharks.

5. An adult male lion weighs the same as two large male leopards.

   An adult male lion weighs _____ two large male leopards.

6. Underwater research is important. Space research is just as important.

   Underwater research is _____ space research.

7. Antarctica is the coldest place on Earth.

   The Arctic isn't _____ Antarctica.

8. The Sahara Desert is hotter than the Gobi Desert.

   The Gobi Desert isn't _____ the Sahara Desert.

2 Read about the animals. Write sentences about them using *as ... as*.

Example: *There are more wild lions than tigers.*
   *There are not **as many wild tigers as** lions.*

1. There are more tigers in captivity than lions.

 _____

2. Forty years ago, there were far more wild lions and tigers.

 _____

3. The Amur, or Siberian, tiger is the largest tiger. The Sumatran tiger is the smallest.

 _____

4. A male tiger is longer in the body than a male lion.

 _____

5. A male lion and a male tiger are the same height at the shoulder.

 _____

6. Male tigers are heavier than male lions.

 _____

7. Asiatic lions are smaller than African lions.

 _____

8. Lions are endangered, but they are less endangered than tigers.

 _____

3 Are the sentences correct? Tick the correct sentences. Rewrite the incorrect sentences.

Example: *An orca is not as big than a blue whale.*
   *An orca is not as big **as** a blue whale.*

1. An axolotl is rare as a giant panda.

 _____

2. Axolotls are less pretty as giant pandas.

 _____

3. A Siberian tiger is as big a cat as there is.

 _____

4. Elephants are as endangered as ever.

 _____

5. A baby panda is so cute as a teddy bear!

 _____

6. People are not as interested in ugly animals as they are in attractive animals.

 _____

Going to, *will* and present continuous

Conditionals

Misshapen carrots

Going to, *will* and present continuous: Talking about the future

We can talk about the future in different ways.

We usually use *going to* for:

• plans and arrangements in the near future.

*I'm **going to start** making my own lunches. Are you **going to try** this food?*

• something we know is going to happen because we have evidence or are certain.

*He's hungry. He's **going to eat** everything on his plate.*

We use *will*, or the **future simple**, for:

• predictions for the future.

*My brother probably **won't eat** this because it looks strange.*

• decisions made at the time of speaking.

*This dish is delicious! I'**ll order** another!*

• promises.

*I promise I **won't be** late for lunch.*

• offering to do something for someone.

*I'**ll take** you out for lunch tomorrow.*

• threats and warnings.

*You'**ll feel** sick if you eat too much.*

We can also use the **present continuous** to talk about plans and arrangements for the future.

*What'**s** the canteen **serving** for lunch tomorrow?*

➔ See grammar box on page 53.

---

1 **Read the sentences.** Circle the correct option.

Example: *There **is being** / **will be** more genetically-modified foods in our fields.*

1. We **are going to go** / **will be** to the new diner in town tonight.

2. It's a hot day. We **will have** / **are having** an ice cream later.

3. You **'ll cool down** / **are cooling down** quicker if you drink a cold drink instead.

4. I promise I **am going to meet** / **'ll meet** you at the station.

5. What **are we planning** / **will we plan** to do at the weekend?

6. Look at that view! I **'m taking** / **'ll take** a photo.

2 Read the lunchtime diary entries. Use the present continuous to write sentences.

George's lunch plans						
Monday	Tuesday	Wednesday	Thursday	Friday	Saturday	Sunday
eat leftovers from Sunday	try new restaurant with Carlos	do class at gym with Sal	have sandwich	go for a run	go out for lunch with friends	go out for lunch with family

Example: *On Monday, **George is eating leftovers**.*

1. On Tuesday, George and Carlos _____ .

2. On Wednesday, George and Sal _____ .

3. On Thursday, George _____ .

4. On Friday, George _____ .

5. On Saturday, George and his friends _____ .

6. On Sunday, George _____ .

3 Complete the sentences with the correct form of *will* and the verb in brackets.

Example: *People **will eat** less meat in the future. (eat)*

1. We _____ more of our own food at home. (grow)

2. Farmers _____ more drought-resistant crops. (develop)

3. We _____ you out soon! (invite)

4. More and more restaurants _____ insects on the menu. (put)

5. Not everyone _____ that! (enjoy)

6. I _____ anything like that! (not eat)

4 Complete the sentences with *going to* and the correct verb from the box.

avoid	be	buy	eat	finish	learn	try

Example: *I've eaten some bad fish and I think I **am going to be** sick!*

1. We _____ at a restaurant in town tomorrow evening.

2. We _____ the new Mexican restaurant.

3. I _____ some food at the supermarket.

4. My father _____ biscuits this week as he is on a diet.

5. We are going to Italy on Saturday. We _____ how to make pasta!

6. Are _____ your supper? I made it specially for you.

Conditionals: Talking about cause and effect

Conditional sentences, or *if* sentences, are sentences which talk about cause and effect.

If + present simple followed by the future simple is used to talk about the consequences of actions. The phrase using the future simple describes the effect and the phrase using *if* + present simple describes the cause.

If we **make** *a smoothie from these old bananas, it* **will be** *delicious.*
If *you* **don't eat** *this lunch, it* **will go** *to landfill.*

If + present simple followed by a present simple tense is used to give advice or set rules.

If *you're hungry,* **don't buy** *extra food.*
If *there's food in your kitchen,* **eat** *that instead.*
If *food* **looks** *bad, we* **throw** *it away.*

REMEMBER

The conditional sentence does not have to begin with *if*. It can be reversed.
This lunch will go to landfill if you don't eat it.
We throw food away if it looks bad.

---

1 **Match the two halves to make logical sentences.**

1. If you don't finish your lunch,

2. If you have some old vegetables in the fridge,

3. If you don't want that piece of chocolate cake,

4. If you don't know how to cook,

5. If you cook too much,

6. If you cook a large chicken at the weekend,

a. I'll have it!

b. you will be able to put it in sandwiches for the rest of the week.

c. you can freeze some of it for later.

d. you can ask for a bag to take it home.

e. you should make them into soup.

f. you won't be able to feed yourself.

2 **Complete the sentences with the verbs in the box.** Remember to use the correct tense.

| be | buy | cook | not feel | share | not want | ~~waste~~ |

Example: *If we* **waste** *less food, it will be better for the environment.*

1. We will make an omelette if you _____ some eggs.

2. I will wash the dishes if you _____ the meal.

3. If you _____ to eat out, we will stay at home.

4. If I _____ my lunch with friends, they will share their sweets with me.

5. We won't go out if you _____ well.

6. If you _____ late home, we'll get a takeaway.

3 **Complete the sentences with the future simple of the verb in brackets.**

Example: *If we waste less food, we* **won't have to** *produce so much. (not have to)*

1. Landfills _____ less gas if we throw less food away. (produce)

2. If you don't iron your clothes, they _____ nice. (not look)

3. If we waste less food, we _____ less stress on the environment. (put)

4. Our children _____ us if we look after the environment more. (thank)

5. They _____ a better life if we act now. (enjoy)

6. If we buy ugly vegetables, there _____ less waste. (be)

4 **Complete the sentences in your own words.**

Example: *If I cook for my parents tonight,* **they will let me go out at the weekend**.

1. If you don't prepare fish carefully, _____.

2. If you live next to a landfill, _____.

3. If you buy too much food, _____.

4. If you plan your weekly shopping, _____.

5. If we ignore the sell-by labels on food, _____.

6. If I am in the countryside, _____.

WRITING

Write conditional sentences about your food and drink habits. Use the present simple and the future simple.

Examples: *If I* **eat** *chips, I* **will** *usually* **have** *ketchup.*

If I **go** *into town, I* **will** *often* **stop** *for a coffee.*

Past simple vs. present perfect

Indefinite pronouns

Houses painted to create a mural in the Las Palmitas neighbourhood of Pachuca, Mexico

Past simple vs. present perfect: Talking about the past

These tenses are two different ways of talking about the past.

We use the **past simple** to talk about:
- something that happened at a specified time in the past.

*In 2009, she **went** to Afghanistan.*
*Did she **make** a film in 2014?*
- something that started and finished in the past.

*She **made** a film called Afghan Cycles in 2014.*
*She **organised** the Streets of Afghanistan exhibition in 2013.*

We use the **present perfect** to talk about:
- something that happened in the past at an unknown time.

***Has she ever made** a film? Yes, she has.*
- something that started and finished in the past but is still relevant now.

*Shannon Galpin **has cycled** in many different countries.*
- something that started in the past but hasn't finished yet.

***She has worked** on art projects in Afghanistan since 2010.*

1 **Read the dialogue.** Complete the sentences with the past simple of the verb in brackets.

A: We _____visited_____ Malaga last summer. (visit)

B: ¹_____ you _____ the paintings by Picasso in the Picasso museum? (see)

A: Yes, we did. I ²_____ it but my favourite art museum in the city was the Carmen Thyssen museum. (like)

B: Why ³_____ you _____ it? (prefer)

A: I love Picasso but I ⁴_____ it had more variety. (think)

B: I ⁵_____ Picasso at school last year. (study)

A: We also ⁶_____ the architecture. (love)

B: Where else ⁷_____ you _____ when you were there? (go)

A: We ⁸_____ the cathedral. It was a real mix of styles. (visit)

B: I ⁹_____ the *Alcazaba*, an old fort above the city, when we visited. (love).

A: Yes, there were so many different ruins. I ¹⁰_____ the Roman amphitheatre, too. (enjoy)

2 **Complete the paragraph with the present perfect of the verb in brackets.**

There _____has been_____ (be) a settlement in Malaga since the 7th century CE. It ¹_____

(change) enormously over the years, but it ²_____ always _____ (be) a

trading post. Greeks, Carthaginians and Romans ³_____ (rule) the city, but big change came

with the arrival of the Moors. They built the *Alcazaba* fortress which ⁴_____ (tower) over

the city since the 11th century. The largest building in the city centre, the cathedral, ⁵_____

(stand) since the 16th century. Since the 18th century, Malaga ⁶_____ (continue) to change.

First, it developed into an industrial centre, with steel and textile industries. Since the 1950s, however,

it ⁷_____ (be) a centre for the Spanish tourism industry, with lots of beach resorts along

the coast. However, in recent years, its long and varied history means that it also ⁸_____

(become) a destination for cultural tourists.

3 **Circle the correct option.**

Example: *The city of Malaga* **(has been)**/ **was** *inhabited since the 7th century CE.*

1. I **have visited / visited** the city last year.
2. We **have loved / loved** going to Spain in recent years.
3. The weather **has always been / was always** good.
4. Unfortunately, the weather **wasn't / hasn't been** very good when we visited Malaga.
5. We **have wanted / wanted** to visit a city with both art and beaches.
6. I **haven't been / didn't go** to Malaga before.
7. I **have been / was excited** about the trip since we booked it.
8. I **wasn't / have not been** disappointed by what I saw.

WRITING

Write a description of the history and attractions of a city or country you know. Use both the past simple and the present perfect.

Example: *Brasilia* **has been** *the capital of Brazil since it* **was founded** *in 1960. Before that, the capital* **was** *Rio de Janeiro.*

Indefinite pronouns: Talking about people, places and things without giving details

Indefinite pronouns are used to talk about people, places and things in general terms, without referring to specific examples.

	every	some	any	no
one / body	everyone everybody	someone somebody	anyone anybody	no one nobody
where	everywhere	somewhere	anywhere	nowhere
thing	everything	something	anything	nothing

- *Every-* means *all*. It is used in affirmative sentences (this means negative structures such as *not* and *never* are rarely used) and questions.
*Can **everyone** hear me?*
*You can see public art exhibitions **everywhere**.*
- *Some-* sentences and questions are generally affirmative. We also use *some-* in questions when we think we already know the answer.
***Someone** has painted a mural on the wall of our school.*
- *Any-* sentences and questions are often negative, or the answer to a question that is uncertain.
*I can't find it **anywhere**.*
*Is there **anything** to drink?*
- Affirmative *any-* sentences can also have the same meaning as *every-* sentences.
***Anyone** can do that! It's easy!*
- *No-* gives affirmative sentences a negative meaning.
***Nobody** came to my party.*
*If you've got **nothing** else to do …*

REMEMBER

One and *body* are interchangeable. *Some**one*** and *some**body*** have the same meaning.
We condense *nobody*, but we don't condense *no one*.

1 (Circle) **the correct option.**

Example: *Public sculptures should be put* (**anywhere**) */ nowhere they can be seen.*

1. **Everyone / Someone** should be able to visit museums.

2. Museums should be free for **everybody / nobody**.

3. **Anyone / Someone** can be inspired by art.

4. The government has spent money on **something / anything** many people don't like.

5. Don't believe **everything / something** you hear about the cost of public art!

6. Not **everyone / someone** agrees that graffiti is public art.

7. Sometimes, **someone / anyone** from a museum has asked for the graffiti.

8. **No one / Anyone** thinks more public money should be spent on art than education, surely?

2 (Circle) **the correct option to complete the paragraph.**

(**Everyone**) **/ Someone** understands art, even if we can't describe it in words. A long time ago, [1]**someone / anyone** got the urge to express themselves with paint on the walls of a cave, and [2]**everyone / no one** could see what they produced. Art has changed, along with [3]**everything / something** else. Now, it can be created out of [4]**anything / something**. In the case of digital art, it can even be created out of [5]**nothing / something** but a computer programme. The British artist David Hockney is mostly a painter, but he also likes producing [6]**something / anything**, such as a quick sketch of the sunrise, for friends on his iPad. This is [7]**anything / nothing** new in terms of technique, but it is still art.

3 **Complete the article with indefinite pronouns.**

I have _____*nothing*_____ to do this weekend, and [1]_____ to do it with! I need to find [2]_____ to go out with! Maybe we could go and see [3]_____ at the cinema. There's that new film that [4]_____ is talking about. Or we could go [5]_____ for a meal. I like to eat almost [6]_____! I just can't think of [7]_____ to go with. [8]_____ is better when you share the experience with [9]_____ .

WRITING

Write a short dialogue between two people who have different experiences and opinions on art.

Example: A: *Everyone has been to an art gallery, surely?*

  B: *Nobody I know has been to a gallery. We all prefer the cinema.*

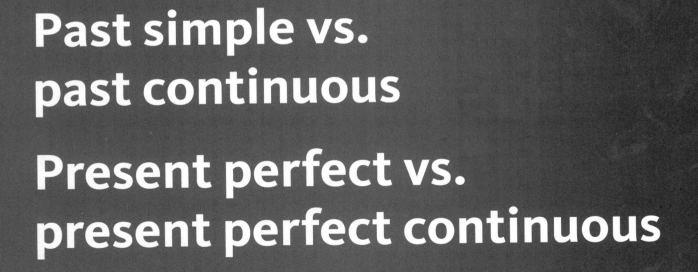

Past simple vs. past continuous

Present perfect vs. present perfect continuous

Photographer Jimmy Chin took this photo of a risk-taking climber in Yosemite National Park, California, USA.

Past simple vs. past continuous: Talking about the past

We use the **past simple** for completed actions in the past (see Unit 4 for more details).
*What **did** the elephants **do** when they **heard** the noise?*

We use the **past continuous**:
* to talk about actions that were in progress at a particular time in the past.
*All the animals in the nature reserve **were making** a lot of noise.*
* to talk about two or more actions that were in progress at the same time in the past.
*The birds **were flying** and the elephants **were running**.*
* for setting the scene of a story.
*The sun **was shining** and the birds **were singing** in the trees.*

We use the **past simple** and **past continuous** together:
* when a past simple action 'interrupts' a past continuous action.
*I **was driving** my car when I **saw** a hole in the middle of the road.*
* to tell a story in the past.
*The day before the earthquake **struck**, all the animals in the nature reserve **were making** a lot of noise.*

➔ See grammar box on page 54.

REMEMBER

We generally use *when* with the past simple: *The storm **was** fierce **when** it **hit** the island.*
We generally use *while* with the past continuous: ***While** we **were sheltering**, the radio **was keeping** us updated.*

1 **Complete the sentences with *when* or *while*.**

Example: ***When** the hurricane reached the island, we were already sheltering in the refuge.*

1. The children were laughing _____ they were playing on the beach earlier.

2. He warned me _____ I decided to go outside again.

3. _____ I was preparing for the storm, my friends were playing in the garden.

4. I was so sorry _____ I heard about the damage to your house.

5. _____ we went back to the beach, the weather was cold and wet.

6. I was watching the news _____ my parents were driving home.

7. I was working on my computer _____ the electricity went off.

8. _____ the earthquake struck, I screamed.

2 **Complete the sentences with the past simple or past continuous forms of the verbs in brackets.**

Example: *They **were eating** breakfast when the earthquake **happened**. (eat, happen)*

1. The sun _____ and the birds _____ when the earthquake hit. (shine, sing)
2. What _____ you _____ when the storm _____? (do, arrive)
3. I _____ the windows when the wind _____ to blow. (lock, start)
4. When I _____ into town the next day, it _____ still _____. (go, rain)
5. He _____ outside when the snow _____ to fall. (sit, start)
6. While I _____ home, it _____ to rain. (run, begin)
7. I _____ the road when I _____ the car. (cross, see)
8. I _____ heavily when the rescuer _____ me a drink. (breathe, give)

3 **Use the prompts to write questions.**

Example: *who / you talk to / when / I arrive*
   Who were you talking to when I arrived?

1. where / you go / yesterday afternoon / when / I see you

   _____

2. what / you listen to / while / you / do homework / last night

   _____

3. who / you talk to / when / you hear / the news

   _____

4. what / you do / when / the police / arrive

   _____

5. what / the teacher say / when / she / see / you

   _____

6. what / your friends do / while / you give / your presentation

   _____

WRITING

Write five sentences describing what you were doing when something else happened.

Example: *I was playing the piano **when** my friend began to sing.*

Present perfect vs. present perfect continuous:
Expressing the duration of activities

We use the **present perfect** and the **present perfect continuous** to talk about things that began in the past and continue up to the present. Both are used with *since* and *for*.

We use the **present perfect continuous**:
- with a continuous, or ongoing, action, or an action which continues to be repeated.
*The fire **has been burning** since three o'clock this morning.*
- with an activity which has finished but whose results can be seen now.
*He**'s been fighting** the fire.* (He smells of smoke and his face is still covered in soot!)

The present perfect continuous is not used with verbs which describe opinions, emotions and senses, even if they are ongoing. Instead, we use the present perfect.
*I **have loved** this music since I was ten.*

➔ See grammar box on page 54.

REMEMBER

We can use the words *for* and *since* with the present perfect and the present perfect continuous. We use:
- *for* + a period of time, e.g. *a month, two days,* etc.
*I've been living here **for** two years.*
- *since* + a point in time, e.g. *last month, when I was young,* etc.
*I've been living here **since** 2016.*

1 **Complete the sentences with the verbs in brackets in the present perfect continuous.**

Example: *The explorer **has been climbing** the mountain for four days. (climb)*

1. He _____ how to reach the peak of the mountain. (work out)

2. We _____ his progress on the Internet. (track)

3. I _____ every update from the mountain. (reading)

4. My mother _____ me not to spend so much time online. (tell)

5. I _____ to her that it is all too exciting to miss! (explain)

6. Over the last few days, I _____ all my homework. (not do)

2 Make the sentences negative.

Example: *We've been trekking for two days.*
We haven't been trekking for two days.

1. I've been wearing these clothes for the last two days.

   _____

2. The group has been arguing.

   _____

3. I have been eating the chocolate.

   _____

4. My companions have been looking for it.

   _____

5. My friend has been feeling very well since this morning.

   _____

6. We have been asking him if he wants to leave.

   _____

3 Complete the sentences with *for* or *since*.

Example: *I've been exploring the Arctic **since** January.*

1. I am with a scientist who has been doing the same thing _____ 1997.
2. She's been sampling ice cores _____ the last two decades.
3. I've been talking to her about it _____ the last four weeks.
4. We've been enjoying the trip _____ we left the base.
5. I've been repairing our equipment _____ eleven o'clock this morning.
6. We've been working on the same thing _____ three hours!

WRITING

Write a paragraph about past and ongoing experiences using the following tenses: past simple, past continuous, present perfect and present perfect continuous. Possible topics to cover: school subjects, sport, hobbies, family holidays.

Grammar boxes

Unit 3 Modals

	Affirmative	Negative	Question
I / You / We / They	have to should can must may might	don't (do not) have to shouldn't (should not) can't (cannot) mustn't (must not) may not mightn't (might not)	Do/Don't ... have to? Should/Shouldn't ...? Can/Can't ...? Must/Mustn't ...? May .../May ... not? Might/Mightn't ...?
He / She / It	has to	doesn't (does not) have to	Does/Doesn't ... have to?

Unit 4 Past simple

	Affirmative	Negative	Question	Short answers
I / You / He / She / It / We / They	discovered	didn't (did not) discover	Did ... discover?	Yes, ... did. No, ... didn't.

Unit 5 Present perfect

	Affirmative	Negative	Question	Short answers
I / You / We / They	have explored	haven't (have not) explored	Have ... explored?	Yes, ... have. No, ... haven't.
He / She / It	has explored	hasn't (has not) explored	Has ... explored?	Yes, ... has. No, ... hasn't.

Unit 6 Future: *will*

	Affirmative	Negative	Question	Short answers
I / You / He / She / It / We / They	'll (will) eat	won't (will not) eat	Will ... eat?	Yes, ... will. No, ... won't.

Unit 6 Future: *be going to*

	Affirmative	Negative	Question	Short answers
I	'm (am) going eat	'm (am) not going to eat	Am I going to eat?	Yes, I am. No, I'm not.
He / She / It	's (is) going to eat	isn't (is not) going to eat	Is ... going to eat?	Yes, ... is. No, ... isn't.
You / We / They	're (are) going to eat	aren't (are not) going to eat	Are ... going to eat?	Yes, ... are. No, ... aren't.

Unit 6 Present continuous for future use

	Affirmative	Negative	Question	Short answers
I	'm (am) eating	'm (am) not eating	Am I eating?	Yes, I am. No, I'm not.
He / She / It	's (is) eating	isn't (is not) eating	Is ... eating?	Yes, ... is. No, ... isn't.
You / We / They	're (are) eating	aren't (are not) eating	Are ... eating?	Yes, ... are. No, ... aren't.

Unit 8 Past continuous

	Affirmative	Negative	Question	Short answers
I	was running	wasn't (was not) running	Was I running?	Yes, I was. No, I wasn't (was not).
He / She / It	was running	wasn't (was not) running	Was ... running?	Yes, ... was. No, ... wasn't (was not).
You / We / They	were running	weren't (were not) running	Were ... running?	Yes, ... were. No, ... weren't (were not).

Unit 8 Present perfect continuous

	Affirmative	Negative	Question	Short answers
I	've (have) been working	haven't (have not) been working	Have I been working?	Yes, I have. No, I haven't (have not).
He / She / It	's (has) been working	hasn't (has not) been working	Has ... been working?	Yes, ... has. No, ... hasn't (has not).
You / We / They	've (have) been working	haven't (have not) been working	Have ... been working?	Yes, ... have. No, ... haven't (have not).

Irregular verbs

Infinitive	Past simple	Past participle	Infinitive	Past simple	Past participle
be	were	been	leave	left	left
beat	beat	beaten	lend	lent	lent
become	became	become	let	let	let
begin	began	begun	lie (down)	lay	lain
bend	bent	bent	light	lit	lit
bet	bet	bet	lose	lost	lost
bite	bit	bitten	make	made	made
bleed	bled	bled	mean	meant	meant
blow	blew	blown	meet	met	met
break	broke	broken	overcome	overcame	overcome
bring	brought	brought	pay	paid	paid
build	built	built	put	put	put
burn	burnt	burnt	quit	quit	quit
buy	bought	bought	read	read	read
carry	carried	carried	ride	rode	ridden
catch	caught	caught	ring	rang	rung
choose	chose	chosen	rise	rose	risen
come	came	come	run	ran	run
cost	cost	cost	say	said	said
cut	cut	cut	see	saw	seen
deal	dealt	dealt	sell	sold	sold
dig	dug	dug	send	sent	sent
dive	dived	dived	set	set	set
do	did	done	sew	sewed	sewn
draw	drew	drawn	shake	shook	shaken
drink	drank	drunk	shine	shone	shone
drive	drove	driven	show	showed	shown
dry	dried	dried	shrink	shrank	shrunk
eat	ate	eaten	shut	shut	shut
fall	fell	fallen	sing	sang	sung
feed	fed	fed	sink	sank	sunk
feel	felt	felt	sit	sat	sat
fight	fought	fought	sleep	slept	slept
find	found	found	slide	slid	slid
flee	fled	fled	speak	spoke	spoken
fly	flew	flown	spend	spent	spent
forbid	forbade	forbidden	spin	spun	spun
forget	forgot	forgotten	stand	stood	stood
forgive	forgave	forgiven	steal	stole	stolen
freeze	froze	frozen	stick	stuck	stuck
fry	fried	fried	sting	stung	stung
get	got	got	stink	stank	stunk
give	gave	given	strike	struck	struck
go	went	gone	swear	swore	sworn
grind	ground	ground	sweep	swept	swept
grow	grew	grown	swim	swam	swum
hang	hung	hung	swing	swung	swung
have	had	had	take	took	taken
hear	heard	heard	teach	taught	taught
hide	hid	hidden	tear	tore	torn
hit	hit	hit	tell	told	told
hold	held	held	think	thought	thought
hurt	hurt	hurt	throw	threw	thrown
keep	kept	kept	understand	understood	understood
kneel	knelt	knelt	wake	woke	woken
knit	knitted	knitted	wear	wore	worn
know	knew	known	weave	wove	woven
lay	laid	laid	win	won	won
lead	led	led	write	wrote	written

NOTES